Fixing Men

Fixing Men

Glenn Diehl

Glenn Diehl
Fixing Men

Published by Spines
ISBN 979-8-89569-066-6

Contents

"To Tyler, Bobby, Aaron, Evan and Fred...my Knights"

Dedication

There are three reasons I wrote this book.
I have been involved with men's ministry groups for over ten years. The first was with the men at Our Lady of Good Counsel in New Jersey. It has been a joy watching them grow together as brothers in Christ. These men continue to inspire me with their dedication to serve the parish and the wider community.
In addition, the Emmaus men's group in Flemington, New Jersey, has been a "rock" during the past five years, especially during the pandemic. Each time we gather, whether in person or online, the Spirit's presence is palpable and doing His work of personal transformation.
Next is the Holy Spirit Himself. A number of times, I questioned whether to finish this book. Each time I was about to abandon the task, the Spirit reaffirmed His desire for me to press on. My great hope is that even a few nuggets of heaven-inspired wisdom are embedded herein.
Finally, in all things, my wife, Mary Clare, has always encouraged me to write. She is the best "ezer kenegdo" I could have ever hoped and prayed for. She is the heart of our family, my best friend, and such a godly woman. The Proverbs 31 woman has nothing on her!

Introduction

The premise of this book is quite simple. Here it is:

> If you fix men, you fix marriages.
> If you fix marriages, you fix families.
> If you fix families, you can fix religious institutions.
> If you fix religious institutions, you can change the world.

But it starts with men. So, a book entitled "Fixing Men." Why? Simply put, because men are broken…only because they're human. Anyone who doesn't think they are or have been, at one point in their life, broken is living in denial. And there's nothing wrong with looking at your brokenness and courageously facing it and fixing it. But first, you have to admit you're broken. At the very least, can we agree we're not perfect? The rest of the book is about how and why to fix us.

A few stats on the "why."

- In 1970, 4% of all children born were born into a one-parent family. As of 2022, that percentage was 23%.
- 93% of all people incarcerated have no father figure in their life.

- Almost 25% of married women who attend a religious service do so without their husbands.
- When a mother attends church, her family will join her only 17% of the time; when a father attends, the family joins him 93% of the time.
- The typical U.S. congregation across all faiths draws an adult crowd of 61% female and 39% male. This gender gap exists in all age groups.
- 90% of American men say they believe in God, but only 33% attend religious services weekly.

One more stat. According to therapist Dr. Phil Mango, who treats individuals and families in any room where men are present, from a football stadium to a boardroom, 70% intentionally expose themselves to pornography at least once per month. Aside from the inherent moral issues associated with this, it points to the more general issue of simply distractions: distractions of the sort that appeal to our lowest base nature and warp our view of others as objects to be manipulated and exploited.

Here's another common society-wide distraction. We all see stats on how much tech-based screen time people spend on a daily basis. My phone actually tracks for me how much time I spend looking at it. Just go to a restaurant and watch how many tables have patrons staring at their phones. Couples sit across from each other, and rather than communicate like humans, they drift off into text messages with people who are not even there! Perhaps they're shopping on Amazon or watching Netflix. Or my "favorite" are the children who stare at their iPad minis and detach from being present to the rest of the family.

And if it's not a cell phone, how about the distractions of sports or gambling (which are an unholy alliance of distraction and greed), or work, or cable TV? There's an entire industry dependent on people addicted to gambling. The radio ads are even hypocritical enough to include contact information for "help lines" if you have a gambling problem. It's like handing a heroin junkie a hypodermic needle and a contact card for the methadone clinic!

Hobbies have created an army of golf widows or families who watch their husband/father retreat into his "man cave" to watch sports twelve months a year. How appropriate to name it the "man cave," where he can hibernate from his family!

Our attention spans are minuscule. We've become an entire litter of puppies who bounce from one thing to another every time we hear "squirrel!" Men are simply part of the rest of the human race, which is now bombarded with options to entertain themselves with banal pursuits that leave us with no brain space for introspection. How about the ability to just sit quietly and think? The pace of life and the introduction of technology are literally crowding out our humanity.

Men are as much victims of the environment as the creators of it. If you don't agree that we're not broken or imperfect, can we recognize that we're at least anesthetized into a stupor from which we need to break free before we can even begin the fixing process? I go to my house of worship and want to scream, "Wake up" to the congregation in the hopes that some would choose to change course and consider living, as Socrates encourages us, an examined life. Perhaps the fundamental goal of getting fixed could be to engage in the process of living an examined, purposeful life.

Dr. Anthony Campolo tells of a survey done of 100 people over the age of 90 who were asked, "If you had to live your life over again, what would you do differently?" Their answers were summarized into three responses.

1. I would risk more.
2. I would reflect more.
3. I would do more things that would live on after I was gone.

As he states, "If we can't learn something from a hundred 90-year-olds, we've lost the ability to learn anything!" We need to slow down and be more intentional with our time.

Men, if we can admit we need fixing, then it becomes a worthy pursuit. The power to change the world literally starts with us.

One last note: there are already countless books on manhood. This book doesn't propose to present anything that adds to the world of philosophy, theology, or psychology. Herein are unvarnished, practical thoughts on how to be a better man in the real world. By the "real world," I mean the world of workaholism, saturated technology, over-sexed media, and countless other distractions that keep us from addressing anything that would bring street-level, fundamental change in how we see ourselves and behave toward others each day. I hope you find something here that brings true change, growth, and transformation.

Chapter 1
Fixing Men

Face it... We're Broken

MOST OF THE problems in the world are caused by men being knuckleheads. Men start most of the wars, embezzle most of the money, abuse most women, and abandon most of the children. Not to diminish the impact of matriarchal societies, which have produced some of their own nefarious women, but inasmuch as history has been dominated by the effects of men making so many poor choices, we have to award the "how to screw up the world" award to the masculine side of the gene pool.

Ego, the lust for power, greed, selfishness, and just plain stupidity are just some of the motives reflected in our history. Men have an innate ability to be stupid. Again, it has been men who have started the vast majority of wars. Men have built and run companies based on the exploitation of their workers. They violate women for their own pleasure and abuse and/or neglect children. Men found religions that create tenets not of self-sacrifice and service but based on control and self-aggrandizement.

How did we get this way? My observation tells me we're lacking positive role models. History shows evidence of families with absent or detached fathers. Children are growing up with little or no positive experiences with men. There's a vacuum filled with people, media, and influences without a positive male presence. Worse yet, sometimes the men in the picture are actually a negative and sometimes even destructive presence. Men are portrayed as misogynists who abuse women and ignore their children. They then raise children who eventually move on to their own families, and what happens then? The cycle repeats itself as these children don't know anything different. When people don't know what to do, they default to what they think is normal. They go back to how they were raised under the assumption that they turned out "okay," so what they learned must be okay, too.

When I meet someone new, and we engage in meaningful conversation, one of my favorite questions is, "Tell me about your dad." The answers are a window into their upbringing and their frame of reference for what a father/husband/man looks like. Sometimes, they reveal deep wounds with scars that have never healed. Other replies, however, are inspiring as they speak of fathers who are compassionate, tender and engaged in their kids' lives. Those people often tear up as they tell of a dad whom they admire and respect. The men aspire to be like their dad and hope to live up to the example set before them. The women reveal a model they hope to meet as a life partner someday.

In some cases, they've already married and met this man. In other cases, they open up about a broken marriage where they thought they had found their prince, who turned out to be a bit of a frog instead. Either way, the point is clear. Men have a profound impact on the trajectory of their wives and children and an opportunity to launch them into a successful future or down a road of immense challenges.

Regardless of our upbringing, we, as men, have the chance to choose our own path. Rather than looking back at the disappointments of our own childhoods, we can look forward and exercise our free will to create our lives rather than let life just happen to us. My experience tells me that a person's view of the past and future dictates their whole approach to every day. We can either look back with regrets for past failures and disappointments, creating bitterness, or we can look backward with gratitude for the experiences that brought us to this moment and gave us the tools to choose wisely. We then either look forward with anxiety for what the future may hold or with a positive outlook for what lies ahead. If you're a person of faith, your view of God's role in your life is likewise revealed. You either look back and see how His faithfulness has brought you to today and then look forward with faith and hope for what lies before you, or, if you've looked back with disappointment and bitterness, you look to tomorrow with fear, anxiety, and a cautious pessimism to guard yourself against God once again not meeting your expectations. Why didn't I get the job or the spouse or the wealth I wanted? Why did God allow me to get an illness or grow up in an abusive home? Your perspective will determine your day-to-day sense of "groundedness" in a foundation you can build on or on a shifting foundation breeding worry and fear. When God comes into the "temple of our heart," first, He needs to turn over the "tables of our sin" and sweep our hearts clean before He can fill them with His Grace.

When I ask men how they're doing, and they reply, "I'm good," I always wonder how they define "good." Whatever is closest to their hearts is often their first response. Work? Good. Marriage? Good. Family/kids? Good. Favorite sports team? Good. Golf game? Good. Our sense of fulfillment is too easily tied to these temporary, material or ephemeral things. We need to anchor to something or someone more substantial and transcendent. Jesus came to reconnect us in a fundamental way to God, who is unchanging. God is the one Person whom we can count on to be constant, dependable, and predictable, to always be good, always on our side, and always working things for our ultimate good. In short, if you're not "good" with Jesus, you're not good at all. Everything else is a foundation built on sand. The old hymn says it best:

"On Christ, the solid rock I stand. All other ground is sinking sand."

Identity - Mission - Destination

If you've hit a "speedbump" in your faith, I think you can view any issues through one of three lenses.

1. Identity – are you settled on who you are and whose you are?

How do we arrive at a view of ourselves? So much is tied to our upbringing, but as we grow and begin to reason, we start to make choices about whom we associate with, what we pursue as interests and hobbies, what we do for entertainment, etc. These choices and exposure to these influences begin to shape our self-image. I think about people who become "Trekkies," attending ComicCon in costume and spending hundreds, thousands of dollars to immerse themselves in that culture. How about people who dedicate themselves to a sport? The dedication required to become a world-class gymnast, skier, or tennis pro is impressive and defines much of who they are. Musicians spend hours practicing their instruments. Involvement in and dedication to these things become part of our identity. If something intrudes into these pursuits, it can rock our world and shake our self-worth. Think of the athlete who suffers a career-ending injury or a musician who loses their hearing. A grounding of ourselves in such an ephemeral pursuit, only to see it evaporate, can derail our whole lives. So, choosing what we do, with whom, and why are important choices.

Once we start to take on even deeper commitments to relationships, the stakes are even greater. Adopting a more permanent role as a husband or father carries such immense weight. And if you're not prepared to fulfill the commitments implied by these roles, it feels like rowing upstream without a paddle!

A lot of people don't leave room in their lives for much introspection. As mentioned earlier, their day is filled with entertainment, work, and general "noise," crowding out time to consciously choose our center. In the quiet moments, how do you think of yourself? I have a theory. When we don't know what to do, or we have a minute to look inside ourselves, I think we default to our heroes. We aspire to emulate the best qualities of who we perceive them to be.

My family are all big "West Wing" fans, the popular TV show about politics. I looked up to President Bartlet, played by Martin Sheen. It actually influenced how I behaved at work and managed my staff. I would often invoke his phrase when I thought it was time to move forward in a meeting by saying, "What's next?" Something about his leadership style resonated with me, and I subconsciously integrated it into my self-image because I wanted to be someone I looked up to. So, who are your heroes? Who do you look up to? When you don't know what to do in a situation, is there someone you "channel" to help you resolve things? If "you are what you eat" then you also become who you admire. An honest look at our family history, the intentional choices we've made, and the circumstances that have affected us to bring us to this point is the first step to then willfully charting the new direction we may want to pursue.

A person of faith looks to the higher power in their life for an anchor, a guidepost. For the Christian, it's, of course, the Person of Jesus. Not the idea of Jesus, but the living, present-tense Jesus Himself. By that, I mean not the Jesus we've been handed by our upbringing and church experience, but Jesus on His terms as He wants to be perceived and related to. Many of us look at our church affiliation and arms-length relationship with Jesus as an "after-life" or "fire" insurance policy! If I show up each week so God recognizes me in church, then I'm covered. When I die, I'll point to my weekly hour spent sitting in the pew as evidence of my true discipleship. What did Jesus say about this?

"Not everyone who says to Me, 'Lord, Lord,' will enter the kingdom of heaven, but only he who does the will of My Father in heaven. Many will say to Me on that day, "Lord, Lord, did we not prophesy in Your name, drive out demons, and perform many miracles? Then I will tell them plainly, 'I never knew you; depart from Me, you workers of lawlessness!'" Matthew 7:22. Whoa, Jesus! That sounds pretty harsh!

Where is the nice Jesus who carries lambs and blesses the children? Bring me that Jesus Who comforts me and doesn't demand a lot in return!

Why do you think Jesus offended so many people when He was here? And that is the right way to describe it. He challenged people right at their core to decide if they were going to create God in their own image and likeness or if they were willing to do it the other way around. Were they ready to let God decide who they were rather than decide for themselves who they wanted to be? After all, God gave us a free will, didn't He? Yes! We have the choice to let God tell us Who He is and how He wants to relate to us, or we can instead tell God to stay in the nice, comfortable, sometimes "religious" box we put Him in and tell Him, "Just behave yourself in case I need you. Wait until I get cancer, or my marriage is failing, or my business is going under. Then I'll call you, Lord, to come in and fix things"…of course, according to my definition of fixing. Until then, don't make any demands on me, and we'll get along just fine."

Jesus didn't come for that. If that was the case, He didn't really need to come at all. We already had the Law of the Old Testament to tell us how and what we had to do to stay in God's good graces. But that didn't work out too well. Jesus came to shake up the old order, to call us back to what was originally intended: a vibrant, personal, dynamic, challenging, transformative relationship with a living God who offers us not to live as scared slaves of a Judge but as a child intimate with their loving Father.

"When the disciples asked Jesus how to pray, He taught them the famous prayer all Christians repeat every Sunday." It didn't start with "Our Judge," "Our Tyrant," or "Our Higher-Power-Somewhere-Out-There." No! The revolution Jesus came to start begins with the challenge to the status quo at the time by teaching His followers to address God Himself as "our Father". Wow! This has to have blown their minds! These simple men of simple faith, trying to live out a devout Jewish life keeping all the laws of Moses, are now encouraged to refer to God as "Abba," the most intimate name a child could call their earthly father.

That same invitation is extended to all of us. The invitation to accept all the ramifications that seeing God in that way implies. We can approach God our Father as a child who wants to please their Dad, climb up on His lap when we're having a bad day, run to Him when we've done something we're proud of, and ask Him for forgiveness when we screw up. That is the revolution Jesus came to launch. No wonder those in His time were so upset with Jesus. They wanted to not only keep God in a box but all those in their congregation as well. "Don't upset the religious order, Jesus." Are we doing the same thing to Jesus? Are we telling Him how we want to relate to Him on our terms? Why would we give up our ability to define for ourselves how we relate to God? Simple...because He came to rescue us.

I was in New York City on 9/11/2001. I stood on the roof of my 18th Street building and saw the towers fall firsthand. I watched those who escaped run through the streets covered in ash. I also saw the firefighters and police run in the other direction into the buildings to save as many as they could.

For me, those brave first responders mirror who Jesus is in my life. I am convinced that if I were the only person on the 110th floor of the towers, and Jesus were the firefighter on the sidewalk, He would have climbed that tower just to save me. Likewise, if I were the only person who ever lived, Jesus would have climbed the Cross just to save me. I would propose that until you are convinced of the same thing—that Jesus would have come just for you to rescue you from the trap of your sins and selfishness, that you're just playing church. You're keeping Jesus in a nice, tidy box to pull out at Christmas and Easter when you need some comfort and advice on how to make sense of a world gone crazy. He didn't give His life to allow you to keep Him in that box, at arm's length, safely separated from the core of who you are.

Once you let Jesus be who He truly is and not the idea of Jesus, your self-image begins to take shape. You grasp the great gift of living as God's kid, a member of the living body of Christ, a member of a royal priesthood. The titles of who we could become are endless, of what we're offered when we surrender our own self-determination and exchange it for who God says we are. Any other identity is of our own making and way short of what He offers us. So, surrender to His Grace, Love, and Mercy and accept who you are called to be.

Remember, Jesus did not come to make bad men good but to make dead men alive. He invites us to be transformed from men of sin to men of virtue.

Let me make an analogy. When you met your wife and fell in love, did it change your life? Mine did in a big way. I was totally smitten. My mom's good friend noted that my wife "obviously delights you." My whole orientation to life was transformed by the intrusion of this wonderful woman who made me see things in a whole new way. I wanted to reorient everything in my life to coalesce around building a future together. And everything changed. My goals and aspirations, activities, and a group of friends are all now realigned with hers. What was important to her now became important to me, and I was willing to change what I had to do to help us reach our new shared objectives. And what motivated me? My head-over-heels love for her and the gratitude she showed for turning my world upside down. As I write this, we're preparing to celebrate our 40th anniversary. As I like to joke (and she hates to hear!), it's been 40 years of fooling the same woman who graciously has allowed herself to be fooled into staying with me through quite a rollercoaster ride!

God wants to have at least the same impact on your life, even more than your wife. Have you surrendered to His overwhelming love for you? Have you acknowledged the fact that, long before you sought Him out, He was looking for you? And once you discovered Him chasing you, did you let Him in or continue to hold Him at a safe distance?

Again, the choice is ours—to surrender to Him or just continue to "play church."

One last thought on this: Don't use your sin as an excuse to refuse His Mercy and Grace. I've heard people say, "Oh, I'm not that good or as good as you," or "I've done some things God could not forgive." So, what you're really saying is that your sin is more powerful than Jesus' blood. You're telling Jesus that His sacrifice was just not enough to forgive your sin, so you'll just choose to ignore Him. Get over yourself! You're not the worst sinner who ever lived. And even if you were, Jesus' blood, even just one drop of it, would be sufficient to save you.

You're looking into the eyes of Jesus on the cross and saying, "I need more. Your sacrifice is not enough to draw me to follow you." How ungrateful! How belligerent! How dismissive of the greatest act of love…to lay down one's life for a friend. What else would you ask of Him?

And God not only forgives us of our sins but wants to heal the scars left by them. We all like the idea of forgiveness: a fresh start, a healing of a broken relationship. When we mess up, it's hard to ask for forgiveness, but the benefits outweigh the difficulty. I recently read a great quote.

"We repent enough to be forgiven, but do we surrender enough to be changed?"

But suppose you're the one who needs to forgive someone else? And suppose they're not around, having gone out of your life or died? You can still forgive them and stop carrying around the anger, hurt, and bitterness. I've heard it said that unforgiveness is like drinking poison and hoping the other person dies. The hurts can be real and deep, but so can the healing of letting go and looking forward instead of back. Maybe it's time to make a list of those you need to let go of. Get them off your back and stop carrying around the weight of unforgiveness.

Once you get through that list, you can now move to the most important person to forgive…yourself. I think we all have a little voice in our
heads accusing us of not living up to our own expectations. The voice
whispers things like:

"You're a failure"
"You're not that smart."
"No one could ever love you"
"You get what you deserve…nothing."
*"You've done some pretty bad things to people, and they'll never
forgive you."*
"God certainly could never forgive you."

The list of these lies in my head can be endless. And when I run out
of lies in my head, the world and the culture feed me plenty of lies about
what success, goodness, and happiness look like. Add those lies to the
lies I tell myself, and I can get pretty defeated very quickly. But what
does God say about me?

Jesus came to speak the truth about Himself and about us.

"and you will know the truth, and the truth will set you free."

— John 8:32

The Scriptures are full of truths and promises that God speaks to us
and about us. We can choose to define ourselves and our world on our
own terms, or we can choose to believe the One who made us. I would
think the person who creates something has the right to talk about what
they made. But we can hold onto the lies around us and the ones we tell
ourselves.

I've made a commitment to live in truth and reject the lies. I've also
started calling out lies I hear other people tell themselves. If I hear
someone say something like, "Life is just a big struggle," I reply, "That's

a lie." It doesn't make me popular, but at least I'm throwing the truth out there to be accepted or rejected. The other person can accept it or not, but I'm not going to; as my friend John says, "Go along to get along." Why let people continue to believe things that are just not true? In the end, God made us, and you are who God says you are…not the lies the world tells us.

If you struggle to believe what God says, you're in good company. Faith in someone is earned over time. Someone asking you to have faith in them must be based on their claim that they're trustworthy enough to do what they say they're going to do. They can't just ask you to have faith in them, to trust them to follow through on their promise. I think Jesus has earned the right to ask for our trust and faith in Him. He answered the question, "Can I trust you?" by paying the price for your eternal life. The world asked Him can you be trusted and He opened His arms as wide as He could on the cross and answered, "This much."

But faith in anyone is a risky business. They could let you down or, worse yet, betray you. Our trust, our faith in anyone, has to be earned over time. But we don't want to take the chance of being disappointed or hurt. That's the risk of loving.

And how do we measure love? I think it can be measured by how much we trust someone. Try this exercise: take out your checkbook, sign 10 blank checks, and make a list of all the people you'd trust to hold your checkbook for you. I could actually come up with a pretty long list of trustworthy people I could trust with my money.

Now, imagine you're in the hospital in a coma and on a ventilator. Make a list of all the people you would trust to make the decision to pull the plug. That's a much shorter list than my checkbook list! Jesus wants to be the last person on our list of someone we could trust. I think He's earned the right to ask for our trust and faith in Him because He's demonstrated His love by giving up His life.

What is the opposite of faith? It's not doubt; it's certainty. We want guarantees. That's not faith. There's always an element of faith that involves trusting the other person to keep their word. Our level of doubt is simply the measure of how much faith we have. It's okay to doubt because that just means we're stretching our ability to have faith.

2. Mission – Are you clear on your mission/purpose at this moment, and have you embraced it with obedience?

Our mission is wrapped inside our identity. As young people many of us had a vision for who and what we wanted to be when we grew up. Some families have a history of firemen or police in the family tree. Their occupation and identity are almost handed to them from the start. It's a badge of honor to follow in the footsteps of generations of family members who choose to selflessly serve the community in these roles. If this is our story, we want to honor and emulate those who have gone before us. There are pictures on the wall of granddad, dad, and brother in uniform. Of course, we want to be our family heroes! But suppose occupations and roles are not so easily defined?

I believe we become who we see as our heroes. If not a family member, someone we look up to shaped our vision for our life's mission and purpose. Maybe a teacher or coach inspired us. Maybe a football or baseball player was our inspiration to pursue a sports career. I had a college professor who challenged me to consider a career in law or even politics. His belief in me gave me the impetus to complete a philosophy degree as a precursor to law studies. Life circumstances took me in another direction, but for a long time, this professor's influence guided my vision for the future. As a person of faith, we exchange our vision and purpose for a surrendered vision of what God may ask us to do. And surrender is the right word. Many of us have been led in a direction we would never have chosen, but the fruit of our lives has shown God's leading to be the best path.

So why do you do what you do? Have you consciously chosen your life's mission, or has it just sort of "happened" to you? Were you handed a vision by a parent or other mentor that maybe you didn't really aspire to, but it seemed like a good idea? Or maybe we didn't want to disappoint those who were encouraging us to move in a certain direction. Your "choices" were maybe not choices at all. Perhaps we all know someone who reached a midlife crisis and completely turned a corner, moving away from a multiple-decade-long career into something completely different. They reached a crossroads of awareness and made a conscious choice to no longer try to meet other people's expectations but instead to engage in their passion. My dad is such a person.

By all accounts, my dad was pretty typical. He grew up as the youngest of five children. His older brother, my uncle Dick, was the "smart one," becoming a pharmacist. Dad decided he wasn't as smart as his brother, so he had to outwork him to be successful. He worked hard, first as a "grease monkey" doing automotive oil changes. Then he entered the Navy and discovered he wasn't as dumb as he thought he was. The way he puts it, he looked around the ship and realized that if he just had to compete with his shipmates in the world, he was going to be okay. Maybe he wasn't smarter than 5% of the other guys on the ship, but he would just outwork them. He raised my brothers and me with the same work ethic. His identity was wrapped up in this belief that he might not be the smartest guy in the room, but he could outwork the rest. I recall virtually every morning growing up with him leaving the house before 6:30 a.m. to go to New York City with a tie on and shoes shined, ready to take on the challenge of the day. His silent example set the bar for the rest of us. He rose to near the top of his industry, eventually becoming a vice president of an international beverage company. And then God intervened...perhaps where He was not initially welcomed.

My mother had a spiritual conversion, coming alive to her faith in her mid-forties. For a few years, she attended prayer meetings and Bible studies, always inviting Dad to join her, but he always politely declined.

Finally, she cajoled him into attending a weekend retreat. He honored her request and agreed to go.

When they arrived on that Friday night, the leader split up the couples and paired everyone with a stranger. My dad was paired with an older nun. As he tells it, the last time he spoke to a nun, he was running away from her in grammar school, trying not to get hit with a ruler! His mind, however, was about to be blown.

After a brief talk, the pairs were to answer the initial question, "When did you ever feel closest to God?" Dad answered first, stating that he felt close to God as a kid serving Mass up on the altar in his altar boy outfit. Then, it was the nun's turn. She stated she felt close to God when, as a young teenager, she was sexually assaulted by a group of men. In the midst of that trauma, she said that God assured her that she would overcome and that the terrible moment would not define who she was. Well, in that one shocking answer, this nun rocked Dad's world! She destroyed all his misconceptions about nuns, God, forgiveness, grace, and mercy. He started crying that Friday night and didn't stop until they left Sunday afternoon. God used that nun to break his heart of stone and start the process of giving him a new heart of flesh. He came back from that retreat truly as a changed man. Not only did his view of God change, but his concept of his life's mission took a dramatic turn.

At that time, he was working directly for one of the most successful beverage brands in the world, reporting directly to the owner in Europe. Dad felt the call to leave his very successful career and enter the ministry. He traveled to headquarters to meet with the owner, one of the wealthiest men in Europe. When he announced his intention to leave the company, his boss asked why. He told him it was for personal reasons, but the boss pressed in. Dad told him he wouldn't understand, but the boss replied, "I'm a pretty smart guy…try me." Dad told him, "God told me to." At that moment, the boss got a look on his face as if to say, "I thought I was God, and I don't remember telling you to leave." That ended the meeting right there.

Dad left the company and eventually became a deacon, serving the church well for the last third of his life. He and Mom moved away from family and friends to pursue ministry to the poor. They sold their dream home and moved into a double-wide trailer. Mom said years later she was never happier than to be "trailer trash," finally having Dad at home following God's leading and building a totally new life vision together.

Dad started a number of new ministries in the community. He founded a soup kitchen, feeding over 100 people every Monday night. He never paid for any food, getting the local supermarket to donate all he needed every week. He never wanted for volunteers. There was actually a waiting list for people wanting to work at the soup kitchen.

He then started an effort in the projects, bringing furniture, clothing, and food to families. At Christmas, he had people in the parish adopt these families and fill their Christmas with toys and much-needed clothes for the children. Finally, he started a divorced and separated group for those trying to recover from the trauma of a broken relationship.

Was Dad perfect? Of course not. But his life is an example of someone whose identity was totally changed, setting him on a totally unexpected path. His story is unique to him, and it is God's call on his life. The choice was his to either surrender his self-image in exchange for a new definition of identity and purpose.

Is your mission, career, or station in life the result of what was handed to you or one you chose? Are you attempting to fulfill a mission you're passionate about or just meeting your obligations? Are you ready to be open to a new mission handed to you by God rather than one of your own creation?

3. Destination – Do you have confidence in the One who promised you a blessed, exultant eternity?

I hate to get lost. What feelings does getting lost evoke? My pulse races, my thoughts start imagining the worst, and if I'm with my family, I'm REALLY stressed that Dad doesn't look like he knows what he's doing! Thank God for GPS. What did we do before it? Well, we often got lost!

Do we really know what happens when we die? There are a few accounts of those claiming to have near-death experiences, returning to tell us all about it. I'm not questioning their belief in their own story, but how does that relate to me? Can I bet my afterlife on their account of what happened to them? I'd rather bet on Someone who has not only been there and back but has offered me a free ticket on the same trip.

God has not only offered an eternal destination but has also provided a roadmap and a pretty good description of what's there. If you've ever had a vacation nightmare (we had a disaster going to Cape Cod, MA, one year), you know what extreme disappointment looks like. Whatever heaven looks like, the issue is more about Who will be there. Even if you wind up in a not-so-great place on vacation, if the company is good, you can still have a great time. I think heaven is less about the destination and more about the company.

It's also the difference between a wish and a hope. Wishes are things that would be nice if only they were true. Disney told us we could "wish upon a star" to make dreams come true. I don't think so!

A hope is based more on a promise. But promises are only as good as the one making the promise. In this case, Jesus is the promise maker and the promise keeper. He came from heaven, returned there in front of a crowd of witnesses, and promises to come back from there someday. Our hope is based, then, on a promise made by One who has made the round trip already! He also created the road map and paid for the trip with His own life. Now THAT'S a hope based on a promise, not a wish.

The key to the promise, then, is being in a relationship with the promise-keeper if you want to receive the fulfillment of the promise. I've been to funerals where most of the sermons and the prayers sound like wishes, hoping the dearly departed somehow wins some eternal lottery. I've also been to other funerals that were more like graduation celebrations, where the departed is heading to a place to see a Person they couldn't wait to be with. One is a somber, sad event with tears filled with regret and wishes that things could have been different between the one who died and those left behind. The other is a joyful "launch party" for a person who has walked through a door into a better state of being. They start a life where they're now more alive than they ever were while on Earth.

For example, when Jesus appeared with Moses and Elijah on Mount Tabor, were those two Old Testament saints alive or dead? I would propose they were more alive than we are now! They were talking to Jesus in their glorified state, already achieving a place with the rest of the saints in heaven. They just came by for a chat with Jesus about what was about to happen in Jesus' life. I can only imagine what they actually talked about.

As mentioned, I was in New York City on 9/11/2001. I stood on the roof of my building on 18th Street and watched the first tower fall. My mind was racing as I started to think through a way to get my staff safely home. It took the better part of the day to get everyone headed in the right direction, either walking across the Brooklyn Bridge or on ferries across the Hudson back to New Jersey. I finally got in my car that night and made my way over the George Washington Bridge back to my waiting, worrying family.

The next morning, it was time to start processing what had happened. As I made my way to church, I was thinking about six clients of ours who died in the towers. I was imagining what it would have been like to be trapped, just hoping someone would appear to take me to safety. I connected the dots to my own life and realized that I had been metaphorically trapped in my own burning building, trying to figure out a way out. And then I was rescued. If I were on the 110th floor of one of those towers and Jesus was a firefighter on the sidewalk below, I realized He would have climbed those stairs just to save me. He is my Rescuer. I was trapped in my own desperate situation and needed a Rescuer to come and save me. Before that realization, like so many cradle Christians, I was just playing church. Until you reach that point where you know that if you were the only person who needed to be rescued, Jesus would have come just for you. I would again propose you're just playing church.

It's easy to play church. You show up on Sunday, put on the uniform, cheer for the team, and if the team does well, everyone goes home happy. You can hide in the stands, fitting in with the other fans of the team. But how many could call up the quarterback and take him out for a coffee or a beer? That's the difference between being a fan and being a disciple and a true follower. Once you meet the quarterback, it changes your relationship with the team. You no longer simply root for the team; you're invested in the outcome and willing to get in the game alongside the quarterback.

So, where do you place your hope for your final destination? In Whom do you place your hope? Here's a question: What is the opposite of faith? Most people would say "doubt." I think it's certainty. What does it say in Hebrews? "Now faith is the certainty of things hoped for, a proof of things not seen" (NASB). Faith looks more like a wish if we put our faith in ourselves or a construct of what we'd like to see be the case. Faith becomes a promise and a certainty if we place our faith in a person who can back up any promises He makes. As the old hymn states, "My hope is built on nothing less than Jesus' blood and righteousness." I'm hoping, believing, and placing my faith in Someone who has earned the right to ask for my trust to keep His promises.

If you're broken, if you're lost, there's a way to get whole. You can hold onto the "rugged individualism" proposed by the American ideal, striving to be the master of your fate, creating a future of your own making. Good luck with that! You might have some version of success as the world describes it. But when the temporal achievements and pleasures of this world have run their course, what will you have to show for it? Is it true that, at the end, the one with the most toys wins? I think not. But it's up to you.

"Secular Virtue"

I'm unapologetically a disciple of Jesus. I've given it a lot of thought and made my choice. However, I'm aware that not everyone reading this may be religious or spiritually oriented in any way. That's fine, but my challenge is to be at least able to identify your basic life principles.

"An unexamined life is not worth living."

— Socrates

Too many people live a reactionary life, allowing their circumstances to determine what they feel are their choices but are actually simply reactions to their environment or other factors they feel are out of their control or not of their choosing. The Oscar-winning film Forrest Gump frustrated me to no end! Who could live by the maxim, "Life is like a box of chocolates. You never know what you're going to get." What a copout!

If you can identify some non-negotiable principles and some unchangeable guideposts for your choices and behavior, then when the challenges of life arise, you'll have a context within which to make definitive choices.

What are these principles, or what could they be? Honesty, loyalty, sacrifice for others, frugality? These are all possibilities. But suppose you're Machiavellian? Your choices may then be greed, utilitarianism, manipulation of others and/or unabashed selfishness. Whatever your principles are, at least be able to identify them and have enough integrity to hold to them consistently. Own the fact that you aspire to create positive virtues or spread vices. Having enough integrity to at least live by your principles will produce their own virtues of sorts, whether religious, spiritual or secular. The world can respect someone who consistently lives by their principles no matter how odious they may be. I can appreciate and respect a person who lives on principle, even if they're an idiot. Better that than someone who doesn't own their actions or conscience, but looks to excuse them based on "its just what happens". Take the time to know what you believe and what guides your choices, and then you'll be ready to create your life rather than be a victim of whatever comes your way.

Armed with a set of principles and a clear self-image, we'll be ready to proactively engage with the future and create good or evil, success or failure, virtue or vice. We, as men, have such a tremendous opportunity to change the world, starting with ourselves and our circle of influence. For those who seek and choose a significant other to go through life with, that relationship is the best starting point to fix the world.

Fixing is Possible

"I don't fear what the future holds because I know Who holds the future."

This is not misplaced confidence because it's confidence not in a political system or even in my own self-reliance and resources. We can look with optimism to the future because, looking back, we can see God's faithfulness that brought us to the present. The value of living in the moment is a proper balance between the past and future.

I find there are two kinds of people. Some look to the past with regret and disappointment in themselves and perhaps even in what God has failed to do with their lives. This breeds sadness and bitterness. Alternatively, looking backward with a view of God's providential hand preserving and leading us to today births a profound gratitude. So, instead of looking ahead with bitterness and fear, we look forward with trust and hope for what comes next. The choice is ours and reveals a lot about our level of trust.

Wounds vs. Scars

Finally, a note about scars: I have two physical scars. The first came from some stupid care of my 12-year-old uncle, who was entrusted with watching 5-year-old me. At one point, he thought it would be funny to lock me out of the house. Everything was fine until I decided to put my hand through the small glass window on the back door! He struggled to stop the bleeding coming from multiple cuts on my right hand, and he definitely had some explaining to do when my parents got home! (As I recall, I believe he blamed it on me!) I carry a lifelong half-inch scar on my right index finger as a reminder.

My second scar was no accident. That was the work of a surgeon to remove my thyroid after being found with cancer in 2006. The scar is barely noticeable, but it's there. The surgery and subsequent treatment were successful, and as I write this 18 years later, I'm cancer-free. (Sidenote: If you get cancer, be sure to get thyroid cancer. It's highly treatable with an almost 100% recovery rate!)

Those are my visible scars. They each tell a story, one of the idiocy of an uncle and the other of a medical success. As I look back at those scars, they say something else. I can either look back with criticism for my uncle's poor judgment, or question "why me?" as to why and how I got cancer at age 47, or I can look at the healing associated with each one. My cancer scar especially tells me the story of my general practitioner, who wisely noticed something different during my annual physical. His experience and wisdom had me with an endocrinologist within days and a diagnosis within a week. Caught early, the cancer was no problem. The scar reminds me of the successful surgery and subsequent healing, not the questions of "Why me?"

But what about the unseen scars we all carry? The rejection, abuse, or criticism from a parent, coach, or teacher that fuels that voice in our heads telling us we're no good and will never measure up? Those scars come from deep wounds. But wounds of this kind are exactly what Jesus came to heal. That's the thing about wounds: they can be cared for and healed, yet still leave a scar as a remembrance of the wound, but without the ongoing effects.

The wounds we still carry, however, are things we need to bring to Jesus. So many people in the Gospels sought Him out to heal their wounds. They brought their brokenness and asked Him to touch them and bring healing and wholeness where there used to be suffering and pain.

Stop carrying those old wounds and the negative effects that come with them. Silence those voices in your head and replace them with the promises of a Savior and a loving Father. As the wounds heal and the scars appear, let them remind you of the powerful healing, and be filled with gratitude for your deliverance from the hurt. Embrace your new identity as one who has shed the lies of the past and replaced them with one who walks in emotional and psychological health. Surrender your wounds and, believe that Jesus has healed you, and get ready for a new and abundant life.

Questions/Action Steps

1. List your guiding principles and things you believe in and would be willing to die for. If you don't know what you're willing to die for, you don't know what you live for.

2. Who are some of your heroes? We become who we admire, so whom do you look up to?

3. Who has disappointed you in your upbringing? Who do you need to forgive?

Chapter 2
Fix Marriages

A MAN WAS WALKING on a California beach, and God appeared to him.

God: You've been such a wonderful, faithful son
and servant. Ask me one wish, and I'll gladly
grant it.

Man: You know, I love Hawaii. I'd like my own
personal bridge, which is only for me, so I can
drive to Hawaii whenever I want to, with no
traffic and perfect weather.

God: That would violate all the laws of physics,
mess up the environment, and cause a whole
host of other issues. It's just too difficult. Ask Me
for something else.

The Man thinks for a moment and replies.

Man: I'd like to understand my wife better.

God pauses for a moment and says…

God: How many lanes do you want on that
bridge?

Okay, let's start by dealing with a few common misconceptions. There's a lot of confusion and a whole lot of angst regarding women being submissive to their husbands. Whenever that scripture (Ephesians 5:22-23) is read in public, you can almost see the steam rising out of every woman's ears! The second part of that scripture passage, instructing men to "love their wives as Christ loves His church by laying down His life," is often glossed over, if read at all. Any wife would submit to a husband who consistently lays down his life in sacrifice and service to her the way Jesus does for His bride, the Church. In the opening verse of the passage, Paul actually starts by advising that husbands and wives be submissive to each other (Ephesians 5:21)... another scripture conveniently ignored by men trying to keep their power and leverage over their spouse.

Ezer Kenegdo

From the very beginning, God intended there to be a loving, mutually submissive creative conflict between spouses. Let me explain. The following quote is taken from the website www.godswordtowomen.org

In Genesis 2:18, God calls a woman an ezer kenegdo, a "helper against him." The great commentator Rashi takes the term literally to make a wonderful point:

"If he [Adam] is worthy, [she will be] a help [ezer]. If he is not worthy [she will be] against him [kenegdo] for strife."

Eve was given to Adam to walk through life together as an equal partner, but also as one who would hold him accountable for his actions. She became an instrument in God's hands whenever He needed to reach Adam. Sometimes, she was a comfort and a supportive companion. Other times, she was a messenger, "calling Adam out" when he was hypocritical in his actions.

I have lived this in my own life. When God needs to reach me, He has my wife right there to deliver the message! My wife holds me to a standard that requires me to live up to what I say I am. Namely, a disciple of Christ trying to be like Him. When I'm succeeding, she encourages and affirms me. When I'm missing the mark (aka sinning or failing), she tells me so and calls me to be better. She is my active "opponent," trying to make me better by challenging me to live up to my aspirations.

My wife has a lifelong friend whose husband died in January 2023. Richard and Cindy were inseparable, managing a successful business career and raising a beautiful family. Richard's cancer came as a shock to everyone, and his multi-year battle challenged the entire family, especially Cindy. As his treatment became more invasive and painful, Richard would (understandably) have his bad days, sometimes losing his temper with those around him. Cindy confronted him one day with one of the wisest statements I've ever heard.

"Richard, we have lived a great life. You have provided for our family, given us an example of a great husband and father, and created memories that we'll never forget. You've taught your children how to live well. Now, you have to teach them how to die well."

Wow! From that day forward, Richard never complained and never spoke a crossword to anyone. He died with grace and dignity, showing his family truly how to "die well." Cindy was God's instrument to reach Richard with the message he needed to hear. However, while he may not have always appreciated the message, he always loved the messenger. Thank God for giving us men and wives as messengers of wisdom and grace when we need it, even when we think we don't!

Why Do We Marry?

People get married for many different reasons. My mom wanted to get out of the crazy house she grew up in. Some people marry to get a green card, for financial reasons or because they want children (only if they don't want to go to the sperm bank, I guess). Marrying is a means to an end. Sounds rather utilitarian, doesn't it? But once those "ends" are met, what are you left with? I don't need you any longer because I've got what I want.

If love is "other-centered," then it never ceases to need the object of loving. In some way, it reveals why God Himself created us. He "needed" to create us because we became the object of His love. After 40+ years, I need to continue to love my wife. The covenant I made years ago has deepened into a central pillar of my life. My commitment to being a disciple of Jesus is expressed first through my living out the commitment to Mary Clare. My faithfulness to her has to mirror my faithfulness to Christ. As much as one human can need another, I "need" her to fulfill all God has called me to.

Here's another unpopular statement.

You, as the husband, are responsible for getting your wife to heaven, not for her happiness but for the spiritual condition of her soul and for providing the best environment for her to develop a deep, personal relationship with God. Of all the things we are tasked with by God, this is the most important. We, however, might list a number of other things we do to earn our husband "merit badge."

Pay the bills
Buy the food and clothes.
Provide housing
Protect her and the kids.
Cut the lawn
Drive her to her mother's house.

I'm sure you could come up with your own list that would make you feel pretty self-satisfied that you've done a good job and deserving of appreciation. But if you fail to tend to her soul, none of the rest matters in the long run. As a matter of fact, she could probably hire someone else to do most or all of those other things. But she looks to you to minister to her, not just provide for her.

How? Again, how does Jesus tend to His Bride, the church? By laying down His life for her. The example He gave at the Last Supper says it all. He, Who was about to give Himself up for the salvation of every soul, started His final meal by washing the disciples' feet. This act of a servant/slave showed not only His humility but also provided us, as servant-leaders of our own family, the best example of just how far we need to go to meet the needs of our wives and families. We lay down our lives every day as we serve those we live with in big and little ways. But aside from any acts of service, we need to go deeper.

If I were to ask your wife what the top three priorities or pressing needs in her life are right now, do you think you would know her answers? It's taken me years of studying my wife even to begin to understand what makes her tick. And some days, just when I think I have it figured out, something new reveals itself. I need to constantly remain a curious student of my wife to ensure I'm meeting her most important needs. Chief among those are the things that feed her soul. Am I doing for her and with her the things that open her up to a deeper walk with Jesus as her Master, the Spirit as her Comforter and leading her to a more intimate relationship with the Father?

We men like a challenge as a way to prove ourselves. Nothing beats that feeling of satisfaction when you overcome an obstacle, complete a project, or achieve a result you've been waiting for over a long period of time. As men, many of us are fixers. (Just ask your wife when she's trying to tell you something, and you want to quickly jump to the end and "fix" it.) For us, it's not about the process all the time; it's more about the result.

Very often, when I'm in conversation with my wife, I reply, "I got it," meaning I know what she's trying to say, and I get the point. "Let's move on" is what I'm thinking. But she's not worried whether I get the point. For her, it's about the process of actively listening to her as she explains what she's trying to say. The challenging word in that sentence is "actively." She doesn't care so much that we're ready to move on to the solution. The act of patiently listening to her is an act of affirmation that she is worth our time and attention. It's our opportunity to validate her as the most important person God has gifted us with, and nothing matters more than not only hearing her but also fully understanding what's behind her thoughts. Can we listen not only to her words but also to her heart?

There are certain roles or attributes that are earned, not self-ascribed. These are things we can't claim or announce but rather achieved statuses conferred on us by others. If we can't get our wife to acknowledge these attributes in us, they're probably not legitimate. Here are a few…

Authority

There is authority that is seized and exercised over people with force or coercion, and there is authority people submit to out of love and trust. Our marriages are an opportunity to exercise authority based on the legitimacy of our service. Your wife will submit to you if she has complete trust that you always aspire to act in her interest and will do whatever it takes to keep her secure in your love for her. This points to the severe damage done by an act of infidelity or a pornography addiction. No one will submit to someone who they don't explicitly trust.

Integrity

No one can claim, "I am a person of integrity." As soon as you hear that, watch your back! That is something attributed to someone by other people after witnessing that person act consistently with their character and show evidence of true virtue. The opposite of a person of integrity is typically called a "hypocrite."

Humility

My dad used to joke,

> *"If I were a little more humble, I'd be perfect. But it's just so hard for obvious reasons!"*

Humility is not self-deprecation but honestly identifying what God thinks of us. If we've been given a talent, then thank God for it. We see athletes do so all the time. I have a musical talent, and I give God all the credit. He wove it into my DNA somehow so I can use it as a gift back to Him and to give pleasure to those who may want to hear the music. There's nothing wrong with identifying your gifts, thanking for affirmation when others see them and giving God the glory for making it part of the unique person he made you.

The question is, would your wife ascribe any of these attributes to you? If the answer is "yes," then you're in a position to exercise legitimate authority in your home, evidenced by your acts of service and spiritual headship. May I suggest you put down the damn TV remote, crawl out of your man cave, store your golf clubs for a season, and actively engage with your wife? Imagine the "shock and awe".

Dealing with Conflict

Because we're imperfect, the conflict between spouses is inevitable. Show me two people who never fight, and I'll show you two people in denial (not a river in Egypt).

Do you know how to fight well? Here's a few simple guidelines:

1. Stay on topic - don't fall into the trap of addressing one issue and then attaching it to others.
2. Don't make it personal - the issue is the issue, not the person's character. If you attack the person rather than address the

issue, you're probably headed to areas that will require a third-party counselor to sort things out (more on this later).

3. Volume and Emotion do not equal constructive criticism.

We, as men, can sometimes default to raising our voices, slamming a door, pounding a table, or some other demonstration of physical dominance. At worst, we become physical and cross that line into abuse.

- If you want to be heard, whisper - This is always a great technique in any negotiation or conflict. It takes the emotional level down a notch and makes the other person lean into what you're saying.
- Listen harder - If your spouse is emotional, try to take a step back and listen. People don't just want to be listened to; they want to be heard. Listen hard for the real issue behind the conflict.

Keep this in mind: I'd rather lose an argument and build a bridge than win an argument and build a wall. Winning an argument with your spouse is overrated. You're not necessarily looking to win. The goal is to reach an understanding of the nature of the issue and then find common ground on which to build toward a mutually beneficial resolution. What's the alternative? Leaving the fight where neither person feels heard, feelings are damaged, and the seeds of bitterness begin to fester.

If you reach a true impasse on an issue or series of issues, it may be time to reach out to a third-party skilled counselor. My wife and I did this a number of years ago and uncovered a host of hurts, wrong assumptions, and blind spots that proved to be the underlying causes of many individual issues.

For instance, I had to identify some attachments to my mother and disappointments with my father that I was projecting onto my marriage. My wife had some issues with her upbringing to address as well. The counselor we worked with had the ability to take a lot of the emotion out of the conflicts and unearth the root causes. There were a number of "Aha" moments for us when we looked at each other and realized the conflict was really not between us but between us, both fighting ghosts from our past. I don't think we could have gotten to those insights without an objective third party helping us individually and as a couple work through the emotions to get to the real source of hurt.

You have to be man enough to submit to this process to move ahead in your marriage. It's not a failure to reach out for help. Often, the bigger failure is not doing so when you really need it.

Let's talk about sex...or, better stated, how do we talk about sex?

The saying goes that women use sex to get love, and men use love to get sex. Unfortunately, in too many instances and cultures, men don't even bother with faking love. They simply force themselves on women in what can only be described as an act of violence. A full explanation of how we got here is a much bigger topic for wiser men than I, but there are a few cultural threads in our recent past that point to an answer.

1. The wide acceptance of birth control began with Margaret Sanger in the 1920s.
2. The sexual revolution heightened in the 1960s and '70s.
3. The feminist movement encouraged women to take on more masculine characteristics to compete in the workplace. (See Pope St. John Paul 2nd's encyclical "On Human Work")
4. The wider acceptance of sexual orientation dysphoria as normative.

In any culture (business, family, society), when you want to effect change, the first step is to control the language. Years ago, my wife and I were part of the marriage prep (Pre-Cana) team in our church. We started the day addressing this topic by asking the participants to describe the act of sexual intimacy. No vulgarity or cursing allowed!

The answers were more tame. Things like:
"Screwing"
"Humping"
"The horizontal mambo"

You get the point. By changing the language in reference to what was created to be an intimate act of self-gift between a man and a woman, you open up the possibility of redefining not only the act itself but also the intent. So, what was the original intent?

God describes it as "the two becoming one flesh." What does that mean?

In their book, "King, Warrior, Lover, Magician - The Four Roles of Man," Robert Moore and Douglas Gillette detail the function of the hormone oxytocin in sexual activity. This is the hormone present when people feel bonded to and trusting in another person. While this hormone is present in great supply in most women much of the time, it is at its peak in men at the moment of sexual orgasm. The rest of the time, most men don't show a high level of it. Women, on the other hand, show a release of this hormone quite often as they engage in meaningful conversation, hug another person, pet an animal, or see an infant…any opportunity to feel empathy and nurturing. Men are wired to experience high levels of oxytocin during the act of sex so that they bond with their partner. Women typically can experience the same bonding experience at other times and with other relationships.

So, if hormonally, there is a confluence at the moment of sexual climax (oxytocin at a high level for both the man and the woman), what does that mean psychologically and relationally? Why did God wire us this way? Is there a deeper meaning and goal to be achieved?

I've coined a new verb in the English language: "othering." This is the intentional act of true empathy whereby you strive to see an issue and experience something from the other's vantage point. What better approach to take than when you're both extremely vulnerable in the midst of the marital embrace?

One final thought on sexual intimacy. I've heard it described best as the renewal of wedding vows every time you're intimate. This can be the case during the sexual act, but intimacy shows up in many other forms.

The Most Important Person

You find out who the most important person is in your life when you get sick.

In 2006, I was diagnosed with thyroid cancer. (Note: If you ever get cancer, thyroid cancer is the "best" one to have. The cure rate is nearly 100%.) The treatment was a full thyroidectomy followed by high-dose radiation. The surgery was scheduled for the day after our 23rd wedding anniversary.

After the successful surgery, I was three days post-op, lying on our bed in the fetal position with a huge hematoma around my neck. At that time, I was also in the midst of a crisis in my business, staring at possible bankruptcy and total loss of the business. Truly, at least circumstantially, the low point in my life. As I lay there, my wife held me like I was a four-year-old. She held me and kept repeating the line of one of our favorite songs,

"God will make a way where there is no way."

I never felt closer to my wife than at that moment. That was the height of intimacy as we faced our uncertain future together, both leaning on God for a way forward. You find out who the most important person in your life is when you get sick. I never questioned it before then, and certainly never since.

Just a note about family planning, birth control, and abortion. Recently, my wife and I were spending a leisurely morning at a beach when three young women sat well within earshot. Frankly, we could not have avoided their rather loud conversation if we wanted to (short of moving further down the beach!). At one point, one of them plainly stated, "I just need more sex." Given their apparent young ages, none of them appeared to be discussing this in the context of a marital relationship. Aside from the initial shock at hearing such a blatant proclamation, it revealed to me what we all know...the cheapening of sexual intimacy between the sexes. I felt truly sorry for her, as she seemed to be reducing her own value as well as that of her potential partners.

While sexual liberation is almost always treated as a women's issue, I think this is fundamentally and equally a men's issue. After all, in one way, shape, or form, it takes both a woman and a man to start a new life. Even if you remove the procreation aspect of sexual union from the equation, sexual intimacy occurs between women and men. Devoid of the possibility of a new life being part of the act, we've reduced the act outside of marriage to a more banal and selfish exchange.

In the early 20th century, when Margaret Sanger promoted the widespread use of birth control, she promoted it as a freeing step forward for women. The implication is that men are oppressing women by refusing access to birth control. The assumption is that men are intrinsically evil and manipulative, uncaring about the place of women in society. If you start from this adversarial point of view, it's easy to build a case. In many respects, you can't blame Sanger for this conclusion. Her efforts were part of the wider suffrage movement, aiming to bring a host of new rights to women.

Regardless of your theological/philosophical/sociological view on birth control, I think the issue starts a bit earlier. Men's attitude toward women and their (men's) commitment to treat women well contextualizes the discussion. Simply put, if we as men treated women with the respect and honor they deserve, the approach to family building takes on a new tenor. How would relations between the sexes be different if men refused to engage in sexual activity unless it was part of a marriage commitment?

Every day, I again make the choice to commit myself to my wife. Each day is an opportunity to renew our wedding vows and reset my role as husband, lover, helpmate, protector, spiritual leader, and best friend. That is the great reawakening of the spark of attraction that started when we first met and, 40+ years later, continues to grow into a warm flame as we face the rest of life together. I'm committed to continually "fixing" my marriage and keeping it in good repair so we can continue to serve each other and sow good seed into God's Kingdom.

I accept the responsibility to lead, serve, and sacrifice for this "special gift" God has entrusted to my care. If she falls short of heaven, I accept that in part, or perhaps even in whole, it's because I failed to be Jesus to her. That doesn't abdicate her personal response to God, but it accentuates the role I accept as the primary caretaker of her soul and the one who can either encourage her to greater virtue and holiness or short-circuit it through my negligence or actual harm. I'm just trying to emulate Jesus.

"Greater love has no one than to lay down his life for a friend."

I think that extends to my best friend, the one I married.

Last thought on marriage is the shortest and one of the best sermons I ever heard. And a measure of every meaningful relationship in your life, including your relationship to God.

"Do I love you because I need you, or do I need you because I love you?"

Questions/Action Steps

1. What three words would your wife use to describe you best?

2. What three words would you use to describe her?

3. If you could change one thing in your marriage, what would that be? Would your wife say the same thing?

Chapter 3
Fix Families

THERE'S a name unique to men. We actually share it with God. It's one of the names of one-third of the Trinity. It's called "Father." What an honor and what a responsibility. When Jesus was asked by His disciples to show them how to pray, how did He respond? He reinforced the role the Father always wanted to play in our lives. Jesus' reply was the "Our Father" prayer. He pointed back to the Garden of Eden, where it all began as a family until Satan made his first attack on the family by tempting Adam and Eve to question the Father's love.

The people we directly affect are certainly the most important, and we want to do our best for them. But even those relationships are limited in what we can do to help them be fulfilled and happy. As one of my sons likes to say, "That's their side of the street." We can support and guide those we love to be their best selves, and let's start by just not being an impediment to their success.

Different Dad Types

Let's start with some good general advice.

> *Fathers, do not exasperate your children; instead, bring them up in the training and instruction of the Lord.*

— Ephesians 6:4 NIV

Regardless of your dad type, the goal is to engage and affirm our families. They are counting on us to provide for and protect them. Lead them with a firm yet loving hand, using the example of our heavenly Father.

I've observed a few different types of fathers. The fundamental categorization is: are you engaged or disengaged? If you're disengaged, the question is, what do you do to hide from your wife and children? Do you hide at work behind the noble mantle of the workaholic father who is just taking care of the family? For most men, our self-image is wrapped up in our work anyway, so being engaged in our work meets a number of personal goals. This is a classic way to hide, as it appears admirable at first as we pay the bills and build our careers. We need, of course, to strike a balance between working to live (and meet our obligations) and living to work (meeting our ego objectives).

Maybe we hide in our hobbies. Pick your poison… gambling, sports, woodworking, music. Most are not bad in themselves, but again, there's a balance between needing a little "me time" and drifting off to these pursuits to avoid actually doing something with our family. And just a note on a more recent phenomenon. What's with the "Man Cave" and the "She Shed"? Have we now institutionalized actual locations to hide from each other? Please climb out of your man cave once in a while and rejoin the rest of the world!

Some hiding strategies are more nefarious. Alcoholism has wrecked countless marriages and families for thousands of years. Addictions of any kind wreak havoc on both the individual and their close relations. The secrecy of addictions to gambling and pornography is especially damaging because they often involve deception as well as the addiction itself. We're not fooling anyone for long. Those closest to us often know more than we think. We're fooling ourselves into thinking we can hide our destructive behavior from those around us, family and co-workers.

It takes true courage to break these generational chains and build a new foundation to pass on to our heritage. There are countless resources to fight these issues, but nothing is more effective than the personal resolve by us as men to commit to a new life of wholeness and health. Some need to "hit bottom" or be "found out" before they either seek help or are forced to do so. If this is you, put down this book and take the first courageous step to getting help.

Many of these addictions are "legacy" addictions, passed on from one generation to another. Maybe you yourself are a victim of an abusive or disengaged father. I have a theory that when we don't know what to do, we default to what we think is normal. We assume we turned out okay so we can mimic how we were raised, and our kids will likewise be fine. We've buried the hurts and disappointments from our own child-hood as a defense mechanism, and we're maintaining our version of "normal" because it's all we know. These wounds run deep and are often glossed over by us just to protect us from facing the pain.

In my own counseling, I faced the fact that my workaholic dad never came to any of my games as a kid. I rode my bike or walked to my base-ball games and didn't really acknowledge the fact that my dad wasn't there to cheer me on. I blocked out the cheers of the other fathers who were there encouraging their sons. For me, it was normal not to have my dad there because his dad was always working and never came to his games, either when he was a kid. I couldn't face criticizing my dad for just doing what he knew to be his job: support the family, love my mom, and take us on vacation every year. He did not have modeled before him the value of quantity time versus quality time.

Once I identified this trend in my father's side of the family, I tried to be more present and more engaged with my own children. Now, I watch my own sons with their families and am so impressed by how they have taken my feeble attempt to the next level. They're much more involved and engaged with their kids than I was with them. It looks like the unbalanced workaholic chain has been broken!

The Drill Sargent

This dad only knows one way to parent..." my way or the highway" and "my house, my rules" are virtually tattooed on his chest. While there's nothing wrong with setting clear boundaries for children and establishing order in the home, how you get there makes a lot of difference. Screaming orders at your family may get results, but those results are more from fear than from true internal character development. There's a saying, "If you want to be heard, whisper." Knowing when to raise your voice versus speaking and making your audience lean in to hear you is an art.

The Cool Dad

Too many parents, and especially dads, want to be the "cool dad" that all their kids' friends want to hang out with. I know of a dad who, long before it was legal, liked to smoke pot with his kids and their friends. Clearly, he was the cool dad! Little surprise, then, when a number of his adult children struggled with drug and alcohol addiction.

In a typical nuclear family, children only have one mom and one dad. They'll have a lifetime of friends but just one dad. One of my kids called me by my first name one day, and I quickly asked them not to do so. There's a very limited number of people on this planet who can call me "dad," and I'd like all of them to use that name. Does that make me "uncool"? So be it.

I think what makes you "cool" is not smoking pot with your kids or letting them call you something other than "Dad." How about being a dad who listens to his children, gives them the time they need to sort out their thoughts and feelings, and patiently lets them process what's inside? Being a dad who is there when they need to talk and just have someone they love actively listen to them. In our house, when we had at one point all five of them home, my wife and I hosted an almost nightly "kid's parade" in our bedroom.

My oldest son once went on a church retreat. When I picked him up, he started complaining about his roommate from the weekend. He reported that his roommate spent almost the whole time complaining about his dad. This teenager had a dad whose communication went in one direction... outward, riding his son about his failures. I asked, "Doesn't he respect his dad?" My son replied, "Respect is earned, not just given because someone happens to be your father. I respect you because you've earned it." He then suggested I give "dad lessons" to other fathers. His offhand comment meant more to me than he'll ever know.

The Strong, Silent Type

Is this just a euphemism for "distant"? It could be. The question is, are you available when your children need someone to talk to? Do they view you as the source of wisdom and comfort, or are you detached from and disinterested in their concerns?

I've heard it said, "If you want to be heard, whisper." There's nothing wrong with being a man of few words if those words are words of love, affirmation, and wisdom when it's needed. The "just listen rule" my wife set down for our marriage also applies to my kids. When she wants to share some of her 30,000 words per day with me, she doesn't want me to jump to a solution before she can fully express herself. Even if I can solve it after just 10 of her words, she may want me to listen to the remaining 29,990 before offering any feedback.

The kids are the same way. Actively listening to them is such an affirming gift. Once they've "got it all out," they're much more receptive to hearing your thoughts. And then it's as important **how** you say something as **what** you say. Very often, less is best. And certainly, don't use this as an opportunity to tell them everything that's wrong in their lives and how you're concerned about what they'll be when they grow up, etc.

When our children were all living at home, we'd have the nightly "parade" of visits to our room. I'd try to get to bed at a reasonable hour (maybe 9:30ish), and then the parade would begin. The kids would knock on the door and ask for a few minutes to discuss whatever was on their minds. Sometimes, it is a small thing, and other times, it is something of great importance. My wife and I did a lot of listening in those conversations, but our availability was more important than any supposed wisdom we might impart. Not sure if I was the "Strong, Silent Type," but we were actively listening and demonstrating at that moment how important that child was to us.

Sociologists agree that the primary structure of any stable society begins with a strong nuclear family. A husband/wife-father/mother team is a formidable defense against a decaying society. A family with both parents properly fulfilling their roles creates an environment of balance and boundaries in which children thrive. All those single parents out there (too often moms) are heroically trying to do double duty raising their children.

I've heard the parenting roles described as the mother as the source of love and the father as the dispenser of mercy. How many of us have heard our mothers say, "Wait until your father gets home," to apply any necessary discipline? This mirrors my very unscientific observation that, from birth to about age 10, the most important person in a child's life is the mother. She provides the nurturing and affirming influence that sows the seeds of compassion and empathy in a child's character.

Once a child gets between age10-20, I believe the father needs to take the predominant role. This doesn't mean the mother is no longer important. Quite the contrary. She plays a vital role in supporting the father's role and stature in the family. I've seen mothers who did not want to or know how to take a small step back to allow the father to step forward. She unwittingly short-circuited the relationship between the children and the dad by holding onto her role too firmly and even denigrating the dad's influence. The result is children who do not respect their father and play the "division game" between the parents. This is the point where parents begin to lose their children as they enter their teenage years. Why?

The father's role in the children's 10- to 20-year age bracket is, for young women, to set the standard for the kind of young man they're going to seek out as a husband. Likewise, the father is setting the standard for what a young man aspires to grow into in young adulthood. This window of time is critical in the children's transition to adulthood, and all too often, the parents do not properly navigate this transition period.

Dads, especially, need to be up to the challenge at this point. Rather than fear the teenage years, parents can embrace this time in the family. The concept of adolescence is actually a fairly recent invention of social psychologists. With the advent of the Industrial Revolution in the early 20th century, children moved away from an agrarian/rural environment to a newly defined time between childhood and adulthood.

For some, as families moved to the city for work, children entered the workforce at a young age to help support the family. They abandoned the goal of advanced education and entered the trades or factory jobs. For those who didn't, they lived an extended childhood focused on higher education as the preferred way to prepare for an eventual professional career.

All too often, the result of extended education also included a sense of delayed responsibility. Young adults, through their high school and college years, were able to delay entrance into the workforce and subsequent independence from their nuclear family. We saw the emergence of adolescence that sometimes started at 12 or 13 and didn't effectively end until someone was in their mid-twenties. In more recent times, due to a variety of socioeconomic factors, we even see young adults living with their parents into their late twenties and even thirties.

The Power of the Tongue...and a Father's Blessing

I met a young man to whom I asked one of my favorite questions, "Who are some of your heroes?" He commented briefly on his own dad, but he was expansive in his praise of his father-in-law. I immediately thought, "How great that this man married into a family with such a great role model." His experience with his own father left something wanting. So much so that when he met his father-in-law, with a point of comparison, he saw character and virtue he had not grown up with. What was so different about this man? He told me his father-in-law had a natural, innate ability to make anyone he met feel good about themselves. He found a way to lift up everyone he met with encouragement and acknowledgment of their unique gifts and abilities. This man apparently has an "other" orientation that focuses on whomever he's with without any need to shift the conversation back to himself. Sounds a lot like Jesus to me.

This points to the broader principle of the power of what we say to either bless or curse. The Bible recounts numerous stories of blessings given or withheld and their effects on the children. The most famous is perhaps Jacob and Esau or the conflict between David and Absalom that resulted in Absalom's tragic death and David's grief and regret.

We, as fathers, can, with even just a word, either launch our children toward a life of success or doom them to failure. We cannot underestimate the power we wield to lift up or put down our children. We need to be careful with even comments thrown out in jest. Our kidding, which we think is innocent and funny, if targeted toward a child, can leave deep wounds. Kids are always listening and internalizing criticisms and can sometimes hold onto them for a lifetime.

The Teenage Years

In our house, we followed what I understand to be the Jewish route. When a young Jewish person has their bar/bat mitzvah, they are invited to join their faith community as a young adult. They culturally move past the mindset of childhood and are encouraged to think more carefully about their choices and outcomes. We loved this idea and attempted to skip adolescence in the modern sense, introducing a simple formula of discipline and independence.

If you use good judgment, you will get more freedom.

If you use bad judgment, you get less freedom.

If you use really bad judgment, I'll come visit you in juvenile detention or jail on the weekends!

If there were some infractions against a house rule, the teenager would get the chance to suggest the appropriate consequence. They, more often than not, meted out a worse punishment than I would have recommended. For example, we had a prohibition against certain forms of music in our house. My oldest son brought in some objectionable music. After helping him recognize why the music qualified as objectionable (a teaching moment), he not only removed the specific album in question but also proceeded to throw out dozens of additional CDs of questionable content. His response was much more extreme than what I had in mind, but I was certainly happy with it.

On another occasion, another one of our kids got a tattoo. Our house rule was, "You can get a tattoo when you get your own apartment or house." Pretty simple. So, when he showed up with a tattoo, rather than turn him into a homeless person, I asked him what the cost of his new tattoo was. The $300 he paid for the tattoo then became his monthly rent for as long as he lived in the house. Eventually, his $300 tattoo became his $1,800 tattoo! His poor judgment literally resulted in a very costly consequence.

This simple formula of judgment and consequence really mirrors the reality the rest of us live with every day. In big decisions and small choices, we all reap what we sow. In effect, our children entered young adulthood at a very young age as they began taking responsibility for their actions.

My wife played a pivotal role in transferring the responsibility of discipline over to me as the children aged out of childhood. She never criticized me in front of the kids and, therefore, affirmed my role as the head of the house and the one primarily responsible for discipline. Her very wise practice of supporting me allowed her to retain her role as "the source of love and support" while enabling me to assume the role of "the agent of mercy." We were a team that guided our children to a place where they could make decisions while maintaining boundaries as long as they were in our home.

Make no mistake, though. We definitely did not have perfect children, and we were in no way perfect parents! When our children "missed the mark" (a euphemism for "screwed up!"), that was our opportunity to show a healthy, proper response. In every instance I can think of, our child brought the occurrence to us without us having to discover it. They were almost always remorseful and penitent, asking for forgiveness. We then made the issue the issue and focused on whether they used good or bad judgment. The resolution then included a direct assessment of the consequences of their actions. When we reacted well, there was, of course, room for disappointment over their poor choices. However, when we reacted best, it was always in the context of love (mom) and mercy (dad). So, even imperfect families like ours can still navigate the worst of circumstances with love, mercy, and grace.

We not only survived the teenage years but loved being a part of every victory, success, disappointment, and hurt. We did it together and grew as parents while helping our kids launch into adulthood. We did so by not abdicating our responsibility to the school, the church or some other source of influence. We accepted our role to set boundaries, enforce consequences, and try to create an environment that left room for growth into maturity.

One thing we avoided was trying to be our kids' friends. I often told them they would have a lifetime of friends but only one mom and dad. My children didn't need another friend as they were growing up. They needed their parents to live up to our responsibilities and help them grow into theirs. I've seen too many parents try to be the "cool parents," only to see their children eventually lose respect for them and push back whenever the father or mother tries to assert their influence. Once you cross that line of compromise, it's hard to recapture the role of leadership and disciplinarian.

Job One – Love Mom

They say the best thing a father can do for his children is to love their mother. As I was growing up, my parents were clearly each other's best friends. I never had a fear that they would split up. They loved my brothers and me as best they could but gave us the gift of a home where there was never a doubt that we were a family because they were a loving, united couple. My dad NEVER spoke ill of my mom, and my mom was my dad's biggest fan. They had their conflicts like any married couple, but they never lingered or were never unresolved. There was no hint of bitterness or disappointment, even during times of disagreement.

I recall when my dad was traveling every other week to California for work. After about four months of this, my mother gave him a clear choice: either he changed his schedule or his job, or he was going to lose her. This was a healthy declaration on her part that, to her, nothing was more important than their relationship. If he didn't feel the same, then they were no longer united in what mattered most. I never saw him more petrified than when facing the thought of losing her.

This seems to contradict what I just said about never being afraid of them splitting up. Even after hearing of this ultimatum, there was never a doubt in my mind that he was going to make the right choice. Needless to say, within three months, he was home every night in a new job role! Good choice, Dad!

That was a big circumstance and life choice he faced. But there are countless ways we make lesser choices every day. How can we, as husbands and fathers, demonstrate to our children that their mother is number one to their father? Kids are smart. They're always watching us to see how we treat Mom. Do we often choose to be with her when we have other options? There's always a place to have some "me time" for us, but are we showing our family by our actions that no one is more important to us than our wife?

We're setting that example of sacrificial love that our children will emulate when they move into their own marriages. I have a theory. Again, when people don't know what to do, they default to what they think is "normal." If normal for them is seeing their dad choose to love and serve their mom, then they will make the same choice. So, hang up the golf clubs for your every-weekend outing with the guys, put down the damn TV remote, and crawl out of your man cave! Join your wife and the rest of the family and show them how much they matter to you more than any self-absorbed activity you might otherwise indulge in.

Raise a Few Knights

My oldest son attended Franciscan University in Steubenville, Ohio. Rather than fraternities and sororities, they had what they called "households." Each household had its own culture and charism. My son joined "The Knights of the Holy Queen," whose members committed themselves to living as modern-day knights. Their charge was to live lives of virtue, honor women, protect children, etc. It was quite inspiring to be with these young men.

My son brought this culture back to our home and put a name to what we're trying to do with all our boys (we have four sons). We found a terrific practical application of this when we took our annual vacation to the Jersey shore. The rules for the boys as they related to the women on the beach were quite simple. We accept the fact that God made women beautiful so the human race would continue. However, we made a distinction between a glance, a look, and a stare.

A Glance – Perfectly normal to notice someone who looks beautiful, although they could often use a bit more bathing suit covering their beauty.

A Look – If I see you looking for anything more than a glance, I'm going to ask you what you're looking at.

A Stare – If I catch you staring, you're going back to the house!

Needless to say, my wife and my one daughter greatly appreciated these rules! They felt honored and protected by us men as we tried to treat all women with a healthy respect. If only some women would treat themselves the same way, much of the temptation would be minimized.

This approach extended to highway billboards promoting the local strip club or gambling website, often featuring a scantily clad young woman. Here, we introduced the discipline of "averting your eyes." This turned out to be good practice for those visits to the beach!

In the undeniably oversexed culture we all live in, we have to be aware of the influence on our young men. As stated earlier, pornography is rampant, and advertisers have known forever that sex sells. And what's with all the ED commercials during what is otherwise a family TV show? Between those and the Victoria's Secret ads, we usually choose to change the channel during any commercials just to be safe!

The subtlety is here not just in the avoidance of visual temptation but in the way we, as men, treat our wives and daughters. Do we show them the respect they deserve and the protection they need from us? The women in our lives have every right to expect us to treat them in such a way that makes them willing to trust us. This extends to our manner of speech, how we serve them, our making them a priority over other people and things, and ultimately, how we value their unique place in our lives. The women in our lives are always watching how we treat them, as are our sons. This is our great opportunity to model modern-day knighthood with those closest to us.

God has no Grandchildren

I'm blessed to be a grandfather of seven. Holding one of my grandkids when he was just 5 hours out of the womb, I wondered how they processed their new reality. In the womb, they were the center of their universe. They physically took up 90% of the space, and, as far as they were concerned, everything was just great. Plenty of food, it's warm, I can rest when I feel like it, and I kick my mom for a little exercise. Then… BAM! What's happening? I'm now in a whole new environment where I have to share the space with billions of other people. What do you mean I'm not the center of the universe?

The shock of the birth process is our first reality check and introduction to our selfishness. That's fundamentally what we need to be healed of. Jesus came and paid the price to gain the right to heal us. Our life then becomes a process of repetitive surrender, laying down our self-will to His will. We become conformed to His image for the purpose of accomplishing His mission, not ours.

I believe the greatest gift we can give our children is a clear sense of identity. Do they know what grounds them? Can they identify their core values and guiding principles? In short, do they "own" their reasons for what they do and how they do it? As a faith-based family, we certainly exposed our kids to a variety of faith experiences. We were homeschoolers, which exposed our children to faiths of all sorts, both Christian and non-Christian. This was quite healthy, evidenced by the fact that each of our children has developed their own unique expression of their faith. Some are more expressive/charismatic, while others are more orthodox/traditional. But they own their authentic faith.

This sense of authenticity is not gained by just Bible memorization or weekly church attendance. Faith becomes real in the home the other six days of the week, where you grind out the application of biblical principles. My wife did a masterful job of teaching our family the difference between saying, "I'm sorry," versus "Please forgive me." It wasn't easy to teach a seven-year-old and a five-year-old to resolve their differences in a healthy manner. But them learning to both ask for and offer true forgiveness has now extended into their own families and the lives of our grandchildren.

The daily application of biblical principles builds a culture of accountability based not just on the parents. The scriptures become the objective third-party reference for good living. But you have to keep it real and consistent.

One of my pet peeves is hearing cursing and overall bad language. When someone in my house would slip, my comment was, "You praise God with that mouth?" (The secular equivalent in my Italian grandparents' house was, "So you kiss your mother with that mouth?"). The biblical principle behind it is Jesus' statement that "It's not what goes into a man that makes him unclean; it's what comes out of him." Addressing this issue becomes much easier when you appeal to God as the third-party authority. If my kids ever objected to us holding them to a biblical standard, the reply was simply, "Take it to Upper Management."

It's not just about pulling the Bible out for discipline. One of my daughter's favorite memories occurred when Hurricane Sandy knocked out the power in our New Jersey house for nearly five days. She has a picture of our family sitting around the kitchen table, reading and discussing scripture by candlelight. It was a great use of our time stuck together in the house. Those teaching moments make the faith real and applicable to everyday life. We're teaching our children that it's not about how well you "practice" your religion but how faith has the ability to transform us from the inside out.

What matters most to us as parents is our children's ability to articulate their relationship with God on their own terms. Their faith could never be our faith. Our goal was to raise and then launch young adults into the world capable of defining and defending their worldview while having that same perspective change them on the inside to be people of character. As we all get older, there is a new aspect to my relationship with my children. They'll always be my kids, but as young adults, we now have our individual faith perspectives that have transformed us from just parent-child to a brother-to-brother/sister connection. In our Christian faith, we now stand before God, sharing the same Father. I could ask for nothing more or nothing better.

Life Beyond the Home

Kids are smart. They not only watch what you do more than what you say, but they look for consistency in your values playing out day to day. The way you treat extended family, especially your in-laws, is noted. Do you speak well of your in-laws even though they come from a totally different culture than the one in which you were raised? If you can extend grace to your in-laws, with whom you have lived for decades, you can certainly offer grace to the more transient relationships.

Like my own parents, my in-laws were not perfect. But I learned to appreciate them for what they did well, not for their shortcomings. We had the privilege of living around the corner from them for nearly 25 years. They taught me how to do family in the traditional sense. Their holiday traditions still resonate with my children, who benefited from years of wonderful Christmases, Easter egg hunts, and my mother-in-law's favorite, Thanksgiving. The monthly birthday celebrations, where everyone was recognized, made such an impact on my kids. Even more important were the more impromptu drop-ins for a cup of tea with Grandma or catching up with Pop while he watched Notre Dame football. I learned to value how the constancy of my in-laws gave my children a sense of stability when they needed another viewpoint on whatever was going on in their lives. They were not showy but a rock-solid presence and a foundation for our family.

As Christians, if we truly believe what we say we believe, then we should be the most optimistic people in the world. We have an eternity that's laid out before us by One who beat death and offers us the same victory. We can live this life to the fullest, regardless of what circumstances come our way. Nothing happens to us when Father God looks down from heaven and says, "Wow…didn't see that coming!" Nothing surprises Him, and therefore, nothing that happens to us should shake our faith.

We have a lifelong friend who, at the time of this writing, is battling ALS. This disease has no cure and is often a slow, degenerative process. But this man has shown great courage and is an inspiration to our family. He is probably the best musician I know, having performed around the world and on Broadway. He was the worship leader at his church for years before ALS kept him from doing so. He is also a Bible teacher and continues to lead online weekly Bible studies. (Our family recently did an ALS fundraising walk in our community to show how much we love and support him.)

While visiting him one day, my wife asked him if he missed playing and leading music worship. I'll never forget his reply: "I played music for years, and I did it well for the Lord. Now, I can lead Bible study. And when I can't do that anymore, I'll do whatever I can until I see Him in person." That's real faith and an inspiring attitude. His example speaks volumes to my family.

Are we projecting a spirit of optimism and hope-filled faith to our children, or are we letting the circumstances of the world's culture around us choke out our faith? So much of it has to do with the perspective we choose to take. I believe there are two kinds of people: those who keep track of everything they've lost and those who keep track of everything they've kept. One breeds bitterness, and the other, gratitude. Can we forgive God when He disappoints us and takes us through trials?

Anyone can have faith when everything is going well: money in the bank, everyone healthy, nothing but blue skies ahead. The way to measure your faith is how you are doing when things "go south." That's when you reap any benefits from your religious practice. Bible memorization means nothing if you don't believe it when trials come. Why memorize things you don't believe? And regular attendance and participation in church activities fail if they don't bear the right fruit. How authentic is our faith if it fails to bring us the right mindset when things get tough? It's at times like these that your wife and children measure you against what you say you believe versus what you show them under pressure. You don't have to be a spiritual "macho man." Times of challenge are opportunities for us to show our family that God is truly real to us and that we're leaning on Him to lead us all forward. We're now leading from the strength of meekness, not weakness from doubt. Jesus was meek in the sense that He knew what grounded Him and where His strength came from, namely, His relationship with His Father, who never failed Him. Demonstrating that same kind of faith in our family leaves more of an indelible mark than a year of Sunday services.

Questions/Action Steps

1. What was the greatest trait your family (your parents) has passed on to you? What was the worst?

2. What virtues have you exemplified and passed on to your children?

3. Is there anything you have not done yet for your family that, perhaps, you would commit to doing going forward?

Chapter 4
Chapter 4 Fix the Church

"The church is a hospital for sinners, not a museum for saints."

The Broken Body

PROPHETS AND PHILOSOPHERS, popes and professors, saints and atheists
have all weighed in on this topic! I certainly don't propose to outdo their
attempts to fix or even improve on what Jesus started. Let's together
focus instead on our role as men in our respective congregations. How do
we effectively engage with our fellow parishioners to make a difference
in our families and wider communities?

People go to church for all different reasons: some out of habit or
tradition, some for the community, some to assuage the guilt they can't
forgive themselves for, and some for the good feeling it provides just
touching the transcendent for a few minutes each week. But we can
become great practitioners of our religion without ever having an intimate relationship with the object of the religion. If the reason for being
there is anything other than gratitude for Jesus coming to rescue you, I
would submit that you're just playing church and are there for all the
wrong reasons. He's not impressed with the length of our prayers or the

outward piety we display for others to see. He wants that inward transformation that reveals a surrender to all He is and wants to be for us.

And what's with the long faces at church? Half the congregation appears to be unwilling to show any joy. They look like they've been sentenced to a penal colony for an hour! Church is where we gather to CELEBRATE, not try to slog through the service so we can survive long enough for the coffee and doughnuts afterward.

The Fruits of the Spirit?

"But the fruit of the Spirit is love, joy, peace, forbearance, kindness, goodness, faithfulness, gentleness, and self-control."

— Galatians 5:22-23.

Most of the congregation looks like the fruits of religion are "boredom, angst, sadness, disappointment, pain, and suffering." Who would sign up for that? If we show our families that we're excited to go to worship with a smile on our faces and a willingness to participate with joy, then we're leading by example. Our leadership can be such a powerful change agent without a lot of effort. By that, I mean just be yourself. Be authentic and transparent with those next to you in the pew. It doesn't take much to lead if you embrace the opportunity to simply show others a little enthusiasm and conviction about what you're doing. Recognize that, in many ways, we're playing to an audience of One; we are there to show our love and gratitude for all we have.

When I was in corporate life, I was asked to lead an informal association of business owners. I found it odd that all these "Type A" personalities were willing to let me lead them. I had no distinguishable skills beyond what most of them possessed, but they were willing to let someone else take the responsibility for the direction of the group. Likewise, the first apostles were pretty regular guys: fishermen, accountants, farmers, and tradesmen. Some might have been "Type A's" (see Simon Peter and Simon the Zealot), but they became followers and, in the end, went from followers to a group of deserters and deniers hiding in an attic.

What happened to change them? Jesus showed up and did two things. First, He gave them undeniable evidence that He beat death. "Put your finger in the marks in my body. Go ahead and test Me to prove to yourself that I am alive and Who I say I am." Second, He gave them the Holy Spirit, a deposit of the Divine nature fused with their souls, to empower them for their mission. It turned this ragtag group of uneducated, frightened men into a mission force that changed the world!

We have that same Spirit! What have we done with it? Retreated into our denominations and created weekly services where we could get fed. We have to like the music, the preaching, the comfort of the seats, and the HVAC environment. We often look for congregations that look a lot like us. We look for folks of the same race and socioeconomic class. God forbid we have to travel more than 15 minutes to get to our church! We might not get home on Sunday for the NFL kickoff if we go to the late service! We create a comfortable and accessible religious experience so it fits our lifestyle. If that were the criteria, the apostles would never have left Israel. Instead, they traveled far and wide to fulfill the Great Commission and bring the Gospel to the ends of the earth.

So, WAKE UP church! Shed the shell we've created to protect ourselves from the discomfort and even risks of actually preaching the Gospel and getting into your non-comfort zone to reach the lost all around us. The Spirit of Jesus is a transformative force that takes regular people and turns them into true modern-day apostles. Once we surrender and are willing to drink deeply of all the Spirit wants to pour into us, Who knows what great things we could accomplish for the Kingdom? He knows!

They say you can choose your friends, but you can't choose your family. That's not entirely true when it comes to the family of God. We have chosen each other as the family of God once we choose to follow Jesus. We need to accept that God often plants gardens of wildflowers, not a vegetable garden with plants in a nice, neat row. Flowers are more beautiful and diverse... like the body of Christ. Jesus challenges us to embrace our diversity while, at the same time, striving for unity.

Unity has its roots in identity. Adam and Eve enjoyed that intimate, familial relationship with God before the fall. After a few thousand years of Israel creating more and more distance from this intimacy, Jesus came to restore it. Once we accept each other as spiritual siblings, it changes our relationship with the church. The church building no longer remains the weekly destination to check in with God and see a few friends. It becomes a weekly family reunion where we gather at the same table to affirm our identity as co-heirs in the same kingdom, bound together as a family sharing the same Father, Brother and Spirit.

We, as men, often want to feel we're contributing to a greater good. We're less inclined to stand on the corner and pass out flyers with a gospel message than we are to pick up a hammer and rebuild a house. We're more comfortable making our contribution to God's kingdom action-oriented rather than rhetorical argument and explicit preaching.

So, how do we serve this wider "family" of church? You have unique gifts God has planted in you. If you're a carpenter, serve by building. If you're an accountant or lawyer, help bring order to the administration of the church. Perhaps you're a contemplative or a great thinker. Offer your thoughts and prayers to the family. Maybe you can inspire and teach others to grow in their faith. Musicians have more obvious talents. Whatever your gifts are, identify them, claim them, and offer them back to His service.

That "great philosopher" Woody Allen once observed that 90% of life was just showing up! Faithful attendance with your family at Sunday services speaks to not only your immediate family but the church family as well. For too long, the church has seemed to be a gathering of women who apparently are there to pray for their absent husbands! I still occasionally see the husband/father sitting in the car during the service, waiting for his family to come out. How ridiculous! And when you ask them why they're not inside, they offer some lame excuse like, "I don't want the walls to fall down if I walk inside." So, I guess your sin is more powerful than Jesus' forgiveness? Get over yourself and get your butt inside with the rest of the sinners!

Everybody Matters

I have a friend, Ron, with whom I used to work, who reached retirement age but clearly did not want to retire. He is one of the brightest, most creative people I know and had plenty left to contribute, but he was just not sure where to do so. He called one day to brainstorm ideas for a path forward. I shared with him something my dad discovered when he left corporate life. I suggested he find a place where, whenever he walked in the room, everyone said, "Thank God Ron is here." He reached out to a local cancer support group and offered his services to help revamp their website. Not long after, he took on the role of webmaster for the group, but eventually, the director of fundraising knocked it out of the park! They were certainly happy whenever Ron walked into the room!

He then picked up his old saxophone, which he hadn't played since high school. After a few practice sessions, he offered himself to the orchestra at his church. They had never had a brass section and were thrilled to have him join. Ron found at least two places where he filled a great need and became a vital part of those communities.

As James suggests, we want to be doers of the Word. Great! Find a place where you matter to the success of the effort and let your gifts flow into the life of the church. And we ALL have gifts to share. When I was younger, I described my abilities as "strong back, weak mind" and was ready to do anything to help. I didn't need to be a Bible scholar to contribute and fill my role.

A few years ago, I was part of a startup men's ministry group. The biggest challenge was getting men interested to meet at all. We don't naturally seek out other men for friendships. We look for activities wherein we establish relationships (softball leagues, golf, various civic groups like the Elks, etc). How do you get men interested in a faith-based activity? My invitation included the challenge, "If you're perfect, don't bother coming. And if you think you're perfect, ask your wife, and she'll let you know for sure." Our first meeting had 15 men show up!

Our kickoff event was watching the film "Courageous" by the Kendrick brothers. This powerful movie was the launchpad for this men's group that's still going strong. After a few months of discussing the movie and reading a few men's books, we realized we had to become "doers of the Word." We decided to offer our service to Good Counsel Homes, a ministry supporting women who find themselves pregnant and often rejected by their families or boyfriends. These courageous women choose life, and Good Counsel Homes offers them a place to live and bring the baby to term, staying for up to a year afterward for job training and placement. They and their children are modern-day widows and orphans. Our men's group saw an opportunity, and when the women are ready to go out on their own, we provide all they need to outfit their apartments with furniture, clothing, appliances, etc.—whatever is needed for a fresh start. This is love in action, and through this effort, we've been able to draw more men into the group. It was living the gospel message that spoke most clearly to these new members.

We experienced another powerful example of the church as a family during my recovery from my cancer surgery. The next treatment step after surgery was an intense radiation treatment. To prepare for this, I had to go on a strict iodine-free diet for five weeks. No salt of any kind for five weeks! This required removing any food with salt in it, which included almost everything!

Another dad in our homeschool co-op went through the same procedure a few years earlier, so his wife knew the food restrictions quite well.

I was struggling to find the appropriate diet foods until there was an unexpected knock on the door. In came this man's wife along with another homeschool mom, each holding shopping bags filled with the best foods for prepping for my treatment. They not only brought the food but also took the time to attach a scripture verse promising health and healing to each item. As I sat at the table unpacking the bags, tears streamed down my cheeks. My children saw firsthand the body of Christ in action. This unspoken lesson still speaks to them.

The foundation of church life is keeping it real, being available, and being open to getting out of your comfort zone. I met a man while traveling for business a few years ago. He was contemplating selling his business and was looking for a "next step" to engage in something meaningful. His business had done quite well, so his perspective was envisioning something on a grand scale, something really big. He spoke of partnering with other people to open a halfway house for the homeless or addicts. His plan included raising money, finding a building, etc. I suggested he find one person to help and experience the value of changing one life. Start small and see how your personal sacrifice and commitment to even one person could change their world.

When Mother Teresa of Calcutta came to New York City to open a local ministry, the press gathered around to hear her vision. They asked her about getting government subsidies, partnering with other established organizations, her recruiting goals, and other grandiose plans. Her simple, profound reply ended the press conference pretty quickly. "We are here to suffer with the poor and help them live and die with dignity." Her saintly focus on changing the world one life at a time was in stark contrast to those used to bloated and ineffective programs. Perhaps if church members thought more on that scale, the church and the world would follow.

There's a mountain of books on how to get congregations out of the pews and "into the game." If people are not motivated by their personal, intimate commitment to Jesus, trying to get them involved is often a series of manipulative exercises to either guilt them into it or draw them into an activity for fellowship. In the absence of a personal commitment, I think these other methods will eventually fail as soon as the ministry work requires real sacrifice. I have no simple suggestion, just a desire to see us all motivated by the right thing, or better, the right person, to participate in the work of the Kingdom.

Questions/Action Steps

1. If you could add one feature or ministry to your local congregation, what would that be? What is stopping you from doing so?

2. What work of the church has had the greatest impact on you and/or your community?

3. What unique abilities do you possess that you could offer back to God and His Church?

Chapter 5
Family With a Mission

THE CHURCH, the family of God, is a family with a mission. We take the love we've found with the family we've chosen and bring the invitation to the rest of the "spiritual orphans" who have yet to meet Jesus and the Father. For too long, we've relied on the professional clergy to birth new family members. This is backward. They are our shepherds tasked with safely leading us to higher ground. But shepherds don't give birth to sheep; sheep do! The laity is best equipped to take the message of forgiveness and grace to those waiting to be invited.

As we look for potential new family members, we typically don't have to look too far. Most of us have a relatively small circle of influence with whom we interact on a regular basis. If we focus on the 50 or so people we often spend time with, starting with family, friends, and co-workers, we'll find ample opportunity to share God's message by how we consistently live. Sometimes, talking about Jesus to a stranger is easier than living the gospel in an authentic way with those right in front of us. Jesus says that even the wicked love those who love them. If we just reach out to those around us who are easy to love, that's no big deal. The true measure of discipleship is how much I love the unlovely.

The world changes but does so within our sphere of influence. They say all politics is local, but so is everything else! How many people do you have meaningful exchanges with on a weekly basis? Twenty? Fifty, maybe? Are you bringing positivity, healing, and joy to those you come across each day? Or are you a source of angst? Therein lies our opportunity to bring the presence of Jesus with us.

Iron Sharpens Iron...But Sometimes Sparks Fly

Here's a suggestion on how to pray for a difficult person in your life: Go to prayer and take them with you into the heavenly throne room. Walk with them to the Father's throne and pray for that person who is most difficult to love. Really pray for blessings in their life, healing for their brokenness, and ultimately for their salvation. Place them on the Father's lap and imagine them resting safely in His arms. Now, the next time you're with that person most difficult to love, you will recall that you've been with them in that Throne room. This ought to change your interaction with and perception of them.

Being Jesus

My lifelong friend, Fr. Pio Mandato, is one of those people who, when he walks into the room, makes you feel the presence of Christ. He oozes the aroma of someone who has spent time in God's presence. Fr. Pio lives alone, practicing a contemplative life. I asked him what he actually does all day. I know how busy my life is and wondered how he fills his days. His simple response was, "Adore Him." He said he spends his days praying and worshiping God for the benefit of the rest of us who are out in the world, bringing Christ to our circles of friends and acquaintances. I jokingly told him to "pray harder" because we need it!

I was driving him home after a visit to my house a few years ago. He had spent the night with my family, including our four children at the time. As we discussed his life and day-to-day, I remarked that I wasn't sure I could live the life he leads. He replied, "After spending the night in your house, I'm not sure I could live your life either!" We all play our part in the church. Knowing who we are, Who we are, and our place in the mission gives us the framework to make a difference in the lives around us.

Get in the Game

As stated earlier, the church has not always done a great job of drawing people out of the pews and into active ministry. We've become too clergy-centric. Wise pastors know how to empower and support the laypeople to understand their gifts and own their roles in the Body. There are some terrific books on how to enliven a parish and engage more of the "sheep" in active ministry. The biggest impediment seems to be pastors who cannot give up control. There is an art to leading and keeping responsibility while at the same time giving up control and empowering the rest of the body to contribute.

By giving up so much control to our church leaders, we've effectively tied our own hands and, by extension, God's hands behind our backs. It's so much easier to leave it to the professional "holy people" to do the work instead of us, the laity, taking responsibility to do our part!

I often tell my kids, "People do what they want to do." We simply need to decide to give God the time, effort, and priority He deserves to be about the business of His Kingdom rather than building our own. The church can then be the change agent the world needs.

Conclusion

What I'm about to say does not apply to the following groups:

- All military servicemen and servicewomen… thank you for your service!
- Police, Fire, EMT personnel
- People in the Trades (Carpenters, Plumbers, Electricians, etc.)
- Medical personnel (doctors, nurses, etc.)
- Coal Miners, Commercial Deep Sea Fisherman, Oil Rig workers…and any other similarly dangerous occupation

For the rest of us men, **quit your whining!** If you're reading this in a Western, first-world country, you live in the most prosperous, secure, and free culture in history. Are you fed up, like me, with listening to the men around you complain about their work, their families, or their boredom? The lack of gratitude from many is stunning! If you're in a circumstance so unbearable, change!

But before you do, think about how good you have it. If you have a job that allows you to support yourself and those you love, be grateful. If you have a wife and family who love and support you, be grateful. If you have options and freedom to choose where you live and work and play and worship, be grateful! And quit your whining!

What has become of taking responsibility for our choices? We've settled into a victim mindset, enabling us to blame other people, our circumstances, or other outside forces for our lot in life. It's time we, as men, embrace the possibilities in our lives and step out in courage and faith.

We're stuck in an overstimulated, distracting culture, keeping us from seeing things as they truly are. God has given us all we need to succeed with this one life we've been gifted. With our identity in solidly established in Him, we have all the security we need to go boldly forward to do His work, love those around us, pursue and create justice, peace and hope. Let's set aside the temptations to feel sorry for ourselves, to feel impoverished or powerless. Let's instead get busy serving Him, loving our families, reviving our churches and changing the world.

I'll close with one of my favorite Bible verses.

"Be on your guard; stand firm in the faith; be courageous; be strong. Do everything in love."

— 1 Corinthians 16:13-14

Watch what happens if we live by this simple prescription. Join me as we walk and work together to be all He calls us to be…and nothing less.

Suggested Reading

"King, Warrior, Lover, Magician" - Robert Moore and Douglas Gillette

"The Jesus I Never Knew" – Philip Yancey

"Unbound: A Practical Guide to Deliverance" – Neal Lozano

"The Way of the Disciple" – Erasmo Leiva-Merikakis

"The Practice of the Presence of God" – Brother Lawrence

"The Cloud of Unknowing" – William Johnston